Get I.T.!

How to Start a Career in the New Information Technology

Authors: Zorina Alliata, Lyuba Berzin, Artem Kharats, Sachin Agarwal

Is I.T. right for you?

Copyright © 2015

Publisher: Better Karma Publishing
www.BetterKarmaPublishing.com

ISBN 978-0-9962897-2-6

Table of Contents

1. About this book series

If the CEO of Google walked up to you in the middle of the street and asked you to join his company as a member of the team, what would you say? "Yes!" or "No way! I could never do that!!" The only correct answer is the former: "Yes!"

I know what you are thinking; "Sure, I'd love to work for Google, but I don't know anything about computers or computer programming." While this may be true, it does not disqualify you from working in the wide-ranging, far-reaching, and all-encompassing field of Information Technology (or I.T. for short). With a bit of hard work and determination, and using this book series as your guide, you can learn the skills you need in the new I.T. You probably have some of these skills already!

This book series explains in simple terms how to prepare for and get an entry-level job in different areas of I.T. This first book is an introduction to the culture, terminology, and thought processes you will find in I.T. It also explains what inclinations and personal interests might be helpful for you as you consider different I.T. jobs.

The remaining books in this series focus on specific job types, and explain how to start your career in that role. Some of the series' book chapters are repeated--and that was done on purpose--so that each book can stand on its own. It also reinforces very basic and useful concepts in the I.T. industry that must be known and understood no matter which career path you might choose. You can also reach out to our website (http://www.getITseries.com/), where we plan to post useful information, training links, articles and tips.

The multibillion dollar I.T. industry is one of the fastest growing industries with a high demand for new employees in every part of the country, and ever increasingly, every part of the world. The industry has grown and changed and now offers jobs for all skills, from marketing to writing, design, content managing, training and coaching. There is a place for everyone who is willing to give it an honest effort. You are needed!

2. What is the new I.T.?

Put another way, what isn't I.T.? Can you send an email or search the web for information? Do you look up information on Wikipedia, or watch videos on YouTube? Do you post pictures on Instagram? The new I.T. is everywhere we look, and we use it daily and routinely.

What do lumberjacks, fast food employees, Google programmers, FBI agents, English teachers, television executives, and nuclear engineers have in common? The answer is the use of computers as tools to progress their respective businesses. Now they may use the computer for completely different purposes. For instance, an FBI agent uses a word processing program on his computer to write a criminal report, while the teacher uses the computer to record student grades. The programmer uses a computer to compile code, while the fast food employee uses a computer to place an order for a meal. But at the end of the day, all these folks use computers to gather information and store it in such a manner that it is easy to manipulate or share with others.

I.T. is not just programming anymore. You do NOT need a college degree to get in. You do NOT need to be a math genius. You do NOT have to be a nerd. You do NOT have to spend your nights eating pizza and coding in bizarre programming languages. You do NOT need to be born with a special talent, like a singer, because I.T. is something you simply learn step-by-step like any other job. Whatever you already are, whatever your natural inclinations are, you can mold that into skills for a computer-related job suited for you.

Some say I.T. can be thought of as a collection of information-based services that work together to produce change in the world. It is amazing how the power of Twitter brought us messages from revolutions in other countries--messages that a few years ago would have never been made public. Camera phones exposed abuse of power; GPS technology located terrorists. Technology is changing the world for the better, and you can be a part of it.

Types of I.T. jobs

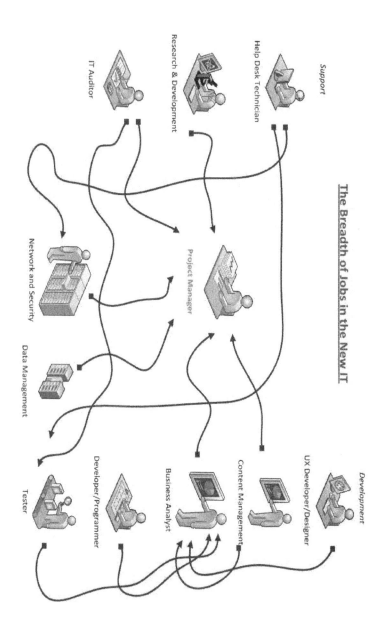

The Breadth of Jobs in the New IT

Support
- Help Desk Technician
- Research & Development
- IT Auditor

Project Manager

Network and Security

Data Management

Tester

Developer/Programmer

Business Analyst

Content Management

UX Developer/Designer

Development

There are many areas in the new I.T., some of them are old and some, such as content management or search engine optimization (SEO), are quite new.

A diagram of most common job categories is presented above. All of them, except for project managers, have entry-level positions available, meaning they could be your entry points into I.T. with little experience.

The lines represent possible career paths; Once you start somewhere, you can always build your skills and move into a different area until you find your perfect fit.

Let's look more closely at these types of positions, starting with support jobs.

Help Desk Technician Also called IT Help Desk or Tech Support, this role provides help to users who are using the company's products. These are the people who you call when your computer doesn't start or when your favorite software program has an unexpected error. This is the most entry-level I.T. jobs out there, and if you can carry a phone conversation and are willing to learn, you have a great chance to get hired. From here, it is easy and very common to climb the ladder to other I.T. positions, based on your interests.

• Research and Development

These jobs are for qualified professionals such as engineers or scientists. In this role you would come up with ideas for new products or processes for your company.

• IT Auditor

IT Auditors help companies comply with laws and regulations. It's harder than it sounds: IT auditors must understand systems, databases and encryption. These are not usually entry-level jobs, although a company might offer training to someone with little experience because these roles are new and there are not enough qualified applicants available.

• Networking and Security

A network engineer is responsible for managing the hardware and software that keep your company running. This could be an entry-level job, if you work at a very small company where the equipment comprises a few computers only, and you learn to fix problems and install software and then work your way up from there. However, bigger companies will hire people with college degrees, certifications and experience for these jobs.

- **Data Management**

Data management is one of the fastest growing areas in the new I.T. Data is a very valuable commodity and everyone wants to collect it and use it, Database administrator, data analyst, big data developer--these are all data-related jobs. You could start small in an entry-level position if you learn to manage a database server such as MySQL or Microsoft SQL Server.

.

The I.T. industry also offers a number of development jobs. For example:

- **UX Developer/Designer**

User Experience (UX) experts make sure thatclients or customers can use the software your company is designing. Job types related to the user experience are user interface (UI) designer, content strategist, and UX developers who write code behind the UI. For those designing, an artistic inclination is necessary; many times they create their own drawings and color combinations. If you are interested in this type of job, you will need to learn tools to design your website, You can start small by creating websites for you and others.

- **Content Manager**

Content managers manage the information their company is making public on its website. They will decide how the website is organized, what article goes where, and how to best communicate the company's message. Writers, editors and people with communication experience might do well in this role.

- **Business Analyst**

A business analyst understands and documents business processes. They are the liaison between the management of the company makimg business decisions and the I.T. teams that will implement new technology based on the company's business needs. A business analyst's role is a great place to start in I.T. It takes people skills and curiosity, and ability to write clearly.

- **Software Developer**

Software developers are also called programmers or coders. They write code for the computers so that users can use them. There are many ways to get an entry-level job as a developer; just learn a coding language by yourself and create a few interesting projects to show your skills.

- **Tester**

Testers, or quality assurance/quality control roles, make sure the company's products do not have defects. In I.T., they work as part of the development team to make sure the code written by programmers works correctly and does not have "bugs" or errors. These roles could also be entry-level, and a common path is for someone from Help Desk to become a QA tester because they are familiar with the product already.

Finally, there are leadership roles within I.T. For example:

- **Project Manager/Scrum Master**

A project manager is responsible for an entire I.T. project and needs to understand all aspects of it. It is usually a senior position; however there is often a need in companies for assistant or junior PMs, so these could be your entry point if this is your area of interest. Scrum master is a new role in I.T., and it grew exponentially in the last years as the Agile methodology took hold. For large projects, a scrum master must have project management experience in order to be successful. However, for smaller projects or smaller companies, the scrum master role can be learned even if you are a beginner.

How Is the Work Organized?

As part of an I.T. team, you will most likely work on a project. What is a project? It's a group activity that has a beginning and an end, and that produces a specific result.

You have done many projects in your daily life. For example, repairing a broken pipe is a project: It has a clear result, a beginning and an end, and one or more persons need to participate in order to finish it. Hosting a fancy dinner is a project. Enrolling your child in school is a project. Organizing a baby shower for your best friend is also a project.

Projects at work are no different. The managers in your company might look at the company's website and say: "Hey, we should really add a page where people can register for our annual conference." That becomes your project scope, or high-level definition of what the project needs to accomplish.

Every project has a start date and an end date. You will have deadlines in your work, and milestones to meet as you move along. No one likes to have a project that will take an unlimited amount of time. You will need to organize your work to meet the deadlines that are set for the project.

The project always has a Project Manager. In most cases, this person will be the one you report to regarding your work on the project. You should keep the Project Manager informed of any successes or obstacles you have in your work. You should also go to the Project Manager when you need help doing your job, whether that means enlisting help to acquire software that you need or help with scheduling a meeting with certain individuals you could not successfully set up a meeting with.

How Is the Project Actually Done?

A common acronym you will hear when it comes to projects is SDLC, which stands for the Systems Development Life Cycle. It is meant to describe *how* the project will be completed, in steps or phases. An SDLC is most times represented like this:

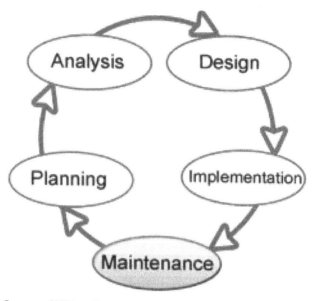

Source: Wikipedia

For example, let's say my son calls me to his room and complains his chair is wobbly, and he won't be able to do his math homework until it's fixed. Looks like I have a new project to fix the chair! What are the steps I will follow to complete this project? My SDLC might look something like this:

- First, I need to **plan** this project. I will ask myself some basic questions. Who is the person who will fix the chair? There is no one else home, so it will be me. When does the chair need to be fixed? Urgently or my son will never finish his homework and will happily use the broken chair as an excuse to play video games. What other projects that I was working on will be impacted by my change of schedule? Well, dinner will be a bit delayed, but that is an acceptable risk.

- I will then do some **analysis** regarding what's wrong with the chair and how I'm going to fix it. Is the leg loose? Can it be fixed by a new screw? Does is need some glue? Is it so broken that I need to replace the whole leg? It seems one of the leg screws fell and got lost in the jungle that is my son's room.

- Once I've figured out the actual problem, I will **design** a solution for it. I am going to need a new screw of the same size, a screwdriver and a bit of glue for extra safety.

- I go to the basement and search through the screws I have left over from other projects. Fortunately, I find one of the same size and that saves me a trip to the store!

- It is now time for **implementing** my solution. I will reattach the chair leg with the new screw and put in a bit of glue at the end. It looks good and solid!

- My son is disappointed he has to get back to his homework, but he does it. I explain to him how to go about **maintaining** the work I've done on the chair: Do not balance the chair on two legs or stand on it.. Also, put it out of the way when he is done working. Good maintenance should result in my work lasting longer.

- Months later, I might notice the chair is starting to wobble again. If that is the case, I will have to start another project to fix it.

The SDLC model has been holding up for most I.T. projects, small and big, over the last few decades. Some use it with a **waterfall** methodology, others with an **agile** methodology.

A waterfall project means that all phases occur one after the other, or sequentially. You will first do the Planning, and you will not start on Analysis until all Planning is complete, and so forth. I used this methodology when I executed my chair-fix project above.

An agile approach means that you will go through the entire process quickly, for a small piece of functionality only, and then do it again and again until the entire project is complete. In the example of my chair-fix project, I could have taken the approach of first tying the chair leg with a string so it wouldn't wobble. This way my son could start his homework right away, so I gain some value. Then later I might add the screw. The next day or weekend I might add the glue. This is an **iterative** way to work through the project.

Both methodologies are currently in use in I.T. Agile has gained a lot of traction lately because it delivers quick value to the users. An agile project will be organized in a certain way. There will still be a Project Manager, but other new roles are defined as well. For example:

- A Product Owner, or the business user who sets the priorities and accepts the product delivery.
- A Scrum Master, or person whose role is to follow and champion the agile process.

3. Is I.T. a good fit for you?

So do you have what it takes to be successful in a job in I.T.? As mentioned previously, a degree in advanced mathematics and a fascination with computer programming are not necessary requirements. Instead, you might be relieved to learn that the skills you need for success you likely already use every day.

For example, can you:
- Write short stories?
- Listen to what people are saying and get at what they really mean?
- Get along with people of various backgrounds and personalities?
- Manage people or projects?

Or, do you:
- Have great people skills and enjoy being around people?
- Like solving puzzles?
- Like building things?
- Like working on a team?

- Like working by yourself?

If you answered "Yes" to any of the questions above, that's great because the skills and aptitudes listed here, and so many more, are needed in the new world of I.T. There are I.T. jobs that will be a good fit for you depending on your personality, skill set and work preferences.

Necessary skills

There is a common core of skills that is recommended for everyone who wants to enter the I.T. job market. Let's take a look at what they are.

Skill #1: Reading Comprehension

Are you able to understand the things that you read? Can you follow instructions from a manual to, say, assemble a piece of furniture you purchased? Did you keep up with this book so far? Then your reading skills are probably adequate for an entry job in I.T.

If you think that your reading comprehension skills could use a little polishing, or maybe some major work, then the best place to turn to is your local public library. The staff there can tell you about reading programs for the public and show you materials for improving your reading skills. You can also use the library's computer, or your own, if you have one, to google 'reading comprehension' and you will find many great online resources.

Skill #2: Numeric ability

We said you don't need a degree in advanced mathematics, but you do need to know some math. How much? For most I.T. jobs, you will need "middle school math." In other words, you will need to know how to add, subtract, multiply, divide and how to solve problems for an unknown. Will you be tested on your math knowledge during your interview for an I.T. position? No. Will knowing arithmetic make your life easier once you pass the interview and get that position? Yes.

If the last time you did "middle school math" was in middle school and you also somehow managed to avoid all math classes in high school and beyond, don't panic. Again, the local public library and the internet have many resources to help refresh your memory.

Skill #3: Logical reasoning

We all like to think of ourselves as logical people. And yet most of us have probably been accused at least once in our lives of being completely illogical--probably by someone near and dear to us, while we were hollering at them at the top of our lungs.

But don't worry. Regardless of what your loved ones may think of your logic, that's not the logic we have in mind. The logic you will need for working in I.T. is most commonly taught in a philosophy or a math class.

The logic I.T. professionals use a lot is the propositional logic; that is, when a proposition is evaluated to be True or False, and then linked to other propositions using words like "and." "or," "if," and so on.

The following is an example of a very simple inference in propositional logic:

Premise 1: If it's raining, then it's cloudy.
Premise 2: It's raining.
Conclusion: It's cloudy.

(source: Wikipedia)

If you think like this, it will speed up your understanding greatly. Very creative people might have a hard time following step-by-step paths from one point to the next obvious one; they tend to jump between ideas and concepts which makes them extremely interesting folks-- but possibly ill-suited for I.T.

Logical thinking can be taught, and it is our opinion that learning about logical thinking will improve your daily life in many small ways. You will find yourself more organized, more thoughtful about the decisions you make, and more skilled at identifying lies and liars. We believe it! Try it and let us know if we were right.

Skill #4: Communication skills

Communication skills are always important and will carry you very far in your career, no matter what it is. In I.T. they will serve you well especially if you want to be a project manager, a business analyst or a UX designer– all jobs where you have to interface with lots of people from different teams and backgrounds.

If your communication skills are just fine but you are a more reserved or shy type of person, there are still plenty of places where you could fit in. Jobs like programmer/developer or infrastructure engineer do not involve a lot of communication with other folks. As a programmer, you could probably spend 95 percent of your time by yourself just coding.

However communication skills will help you in any of these jobs. You need to clearly understand the assignment, clearly understand the boundaries between teams and projects, clearly make your point to explain your decisions no matter whether you are a programmer or a business analyst or a tester.

Good communication skills will help you do your job well and be appreciated by your manager.

So is I.T. a good fit for you?

We made a simple drawing to give you an idea where your natural tendencies might take you in the new I.T.:

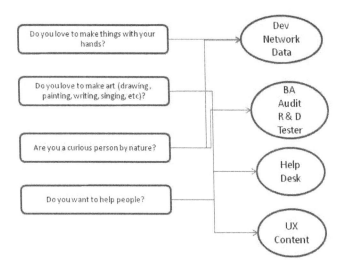

But do not let this limit your imagination. Sometimes the best programmers are those with a big creative bone; and sometimes the best business analysts are those who think in technical terms. If you feel a certain job resonates with you, then by all means pursue it.

Living the I.T. Lifestyle

The dress code for I.T. jobs is similar to any other office job. In most situations you will probably be fine wearing what is called "business casual" clothes. For men, this means slacks and a dress shirt--no tie, no jacket. For women, trousers or skirts and dress shirts or blouses. In some environments, you might be asked to dress casually; this means you can wear jeans and t-shirts. In other environments, you might be required to dress business formal, which means wearing a suit.

To invest in a simple but efficient wardrobe for business casual offices, follow these simple rules:

- Get two pairs of fabric dress pants, either both black or one black and one navy or brown.
- Get a few solid-color dress shirts in beige, blue or white, or a light pastel. If you are a woman, buy a couple of simple jersey blouses that are washable.
- If you are a man, get comfortable but dressy shoes and a belt in the same color. If you are a woman, get a pair of flats and a pair of pumps that go with the other clothes.
- If you are a woman, get a cheap but colorful scarf and a few simple jewelry pieces, like a necklace, earrings or a bracelet. The jewelry should be small and neutral, without any overt

messages like crosses or hearts. Silver jewelry looks elegant, and it isrelatively inexpensive. These clothes should hold you for the first few weeks, until you figure out the office dress code and expectations--and until you get your first paycheck.

The main rule is to always try and look the best that you can. Have your hair brushed, your nails clean and cut nicely, and wear clean clothes every day. A friendly smile and a confident look will complete the picture you will project.

You can find free business outfits at charities like Dress for Success. You can also find inexpensive business attire at discount retailers like Marshalls, Kmart, or TJ Maxx.

Behaving Like a Professional

Once you join a company, no matter how big or small, you are expected and obligated to behave professionally. This means, first and foremost, do not talk bad about the company inside or outside the office. Do not comment about your company on Facebook or other social media. Do not post details about the exact work you do, and do not discuss your salary with anyone but your boss and the human resources department.

Your manager (your boss) is the one you should pay the most attention to. Your manager is the one who will evaluate your wok, decide whether you are doing a good job and recommend you for a promotion or salary increase. Be loyal to your boss and your team, and strive to be a reliable and trustworthy team member.

There are usually rules to follow when working in an office. Many companies have an employee handbook that explains these rules. You will receive a copy of this book when hired, and you should read it so you understand your rights,

Most common rules refer to things like what to wear in the office, how to speak professionally without using foul language, how to treat your coworkers with respect, and so forth.

You will make friends at the office, but remember that most people will remain acquaintances only. You should not gossip or over-share your personal business at work -- keep that for your personal friends and family.

Religion, income, race, age are things you should not discuss with coworkers. A joke that might seem funny to you could offend someone of a different background.

If you are the one who is offended by discriminatory comments or behavior, you must inform your manager and the human resources department as well.

Life in the office is complicated - and then your child's principal calls

You will most probably have a computer (or more) in your cubicle or office. You will have a phone. You must use these for work and for little else. Most companies understand that their workers periodically will check their personal email during work hours, and they are understanding of that, but not if you spend a lot of time surfing the web or looking at illegal websites.

One rule of thumb: Remember that your company logs each and every action that you take online. You should assume you have no privacy at work.

Life is in office is its own micro cosmos, and if differs from company to company. In most places you will find basic accommodations (e.g., bathrooms, a kitchen with a refrigerator and a microwave, vending machines, and sometimes free coffee or tea).

To save money at first you might consider bringing your lunch from home. Leftovers from last night's dinner, a salad, a sandwich and chips, or canned soup and crackers are cheap options.

Some offices have a cafeteria where you can buy breakfast and lunch. A cafeteria lunch can cost between $5 and $10, and the quality varies greatly.

It is common to have lunch with your coworkers, You can ask someone if they want to have lunch together, and start from there. It will give you an opportunity to connect with and get to know your coworkers better.

In case of an emergency call from your kids' school, or if you have an appointment, you can take accrued time off - a few hours or an entire day. All you need to do is to inform your manager and your team, so they can plan their work while you are out.

Life in the office is not too bad, as long as you follow a few simple rules and understand your rights.

4. START YOUR CAREER IN I.T.

Create your I.T. persona

You are starting anew. Whoever you were before, you now have to project a different image. Follow these simple steps to get there:

Go ahead and <u>take a selfie</u>. But do your hair nicely first, and make sure you look good. If you feel you need a professional photo, there are many low-cost studios–some located in retail stores at the local mall–through which to schedule a sitting. This picture must be scanned into your phone and computer.

<u>Create your website</u>. Most I.T. folks basically live online. They invented the Internet and they use it for everything. If you want to be part of that crowd, you need to build yourself a presence online.

A simple website (HTML only) can be obtained for free from Yahoo or other providers. If you are willing to pay a few dollars a month, you can contract with a hosting company and buy a cheap domain name and website with minimum capabilities.

Put your resume and your photo on your website, and a cartoon sign that says "For Hire" in large font at the top. You do not want to be subtle about your intentions.

Next, create a blog, which can be hosted for free by a number of providers. Start blogging about the job you want, the interest you have in it, any news or commentary about the profession that you find interesting. Link your blog to your website so people can easily find it.

Get into <u>social media</u>. Create a Twitter account. Twitter is a great tool - it is very democratic, in that it can put you in touch with celebrities, CEOs, and recruiters if your tweet is good enough. Tweet often (articles, news, commentary about the profession you want to get into), and link back to anyone who pays attention to you. Build an audience - it's easy on Twitter. If you don't know what to tweet, just re-tweet other interesting posts.

<u>Write your resume</u>. Whatever career you had should now be relegated to the bottom of the page, and its description drastically reduced. You are not applying for those types of jobs anymore, so no need to get into

excruciating detail about your old duties. Instead, highlight as much as you can of the work you've been doing to learn your new job. Anything counts - volunteer work, internships, personal projects, membership in professional associations.

Use this format to guide you:

Joe Smith
555-678-890
Joe.smith@email.com
www.JoeSmithWebsite.com

Skills
- Business Analysis, Website Management, Agile
- Software: InDesign, HTML5, Drupal, Rally
- Office tools: MS Word, Access, Excel, Visio, PowerPoint

Experience
JoeSmithWebsite.com
- Created website using HTML5 and InDesign.
- Created and managed content using Drupal.
- Created a blog about Business Analysis trends and developments, updated weekly. Updates are automatically synced to my Twitter account and my other social media sites.
- Posted articles, links, opinions about Business Analysis on social media, including LinkedIn, Twitter and Facebook. Currently have 2,400 followers.
- Conducted business analysis for a project at my church, and created a sub-site for the project. Used Rally to document the user stories and keep track of their implementation.

Regional Association for Business Analysts
- Volunteered as database administrator and website manager.
- Maintained the member database, kept track of membership fees and refunds.
- Created and updated content on the association's website, managed web pages and user permissions.
- Participated in sessions to gather requirements for a website developed using Agile methodology

O'Connell's Bar and Grill, 2013-present
- Served as Bartender. Recognized for professionalism, strong relationship building and quick thinking. Employee of the month for two months in a row, 2014.

Education
- Clarksburg High School, 1989
- I.T. Business Analyst certification from Coursera, 2015
- Active member of Regional Association of Business Analysts

With your online profile all set up, you are now ready to network!

Networking

As you begin your journey into the Information Technology world and gather information to make your entry into I.T. a success, you will hear the word 'networking' quite often. Business networking refers to like-minded groups that perform activities together to build new relationships and learn from each other.

In the past, networking was known as industry executives 'rubbing elbows' with each other to meet potential clients, using sale strategies and thus closing business deals. But due to the social media boom, business networking has evolved to where millions of people are using networking sites not only to create new business but to share their knowledge of technologies, software, I.T. methodologies and I.T. disciplines. The great thing about networking is that you don't have to be a senior-level executive or own a business to participate. Anyone interested in networking with a purpose is welcome to network!

Family & Friends

Family and friends are the first groups you should approach when planning to enter the I.T. workforce. Approaching family and friends is the easiest and most beneficial for several reasons:

- They will be honest with you.
- They will provide advice and details about the steps they took in their career.
- They might know of an available job they can recommend you for.

Do not limit yourself to just your best friends. Ask anyone you know. Prepare a short speech about the job you are interested in getting, and a short summary of the skills you've acquired. Tell folks you are looking: You never know who might have heard of an open position that matches your desires.

LinkedIn.com

More than 300 million people use LinkedIn.com to network within their profession. This is the place to be seen if you want a professional job, especially in I.T.

It is free to join. Set up your profile carefully! Pick and choose what you want to show from your resume. You are not obligated to reveal every job you ever had. Choose your skills. Upload your photo.

Next, look for connections. LinkedIn will help you locate old co-workers or friends from your address book. Join groups based on the I.T. profession you are looking to get into. Participate in any events the groups have, if possible.

LinkedIn works great as a networking tool, but you have to do your part. Be active, participate in group discussions, post links to your blog if you have an interesting article that day.

Try joining Meetup.com as well. Although much smaller, it is an interesting concept and it can connect you directly with people working in your area of interest.

Where the Jobs Are

I.T. jobs are everywhere. Go to any major website, like CNN.com, and somewhere on the right-hand side, a job listing will appear. Looking for Java programmer in Chicago! Many of the job announcements even have exclamation signs in them to convey a desperate sense of urgency.

There are simply not enough candidates for all the available jobs. That's why you have a great chance to get into the industry, and obtain a good middle-class job that is safe and comfortable, and pays very well.

There are many reasons this happened, but one of the important ones is simply that technology is an innovation and as such, it disrupted entire industries. Manufacturing shrunk due to massive automation; journalism shrunk due to online competition from individuals who now have the means to freely create content.

It is hard for folks caught in the middle of this to adapt; not everyone is adventurous enough or can afford to take classes to easily learn new technology. A lot of people were displaced by I.T., and yet I.T. is starving for people to hire! Hopefully, this book series will help bridge some of that gap.

To find the jobs, start with the large job boards. Create a profile and upload your resume on Monster.com, Dice.com, and Indeed.com--all known for their large numbers of available technical job postings. Make your resume 'searchable' so headhunters can find you.

Our favorite method for finding a job is to go directly to companies we're interested in.

Find companies you like, or that have offices in your town, and apply directly on their websites.

When applying for jobs, tailor your resume slightly to accentuate the requirements for each specific job. Do not just blindly send the same resume for every job. For example, if a job posting specifically references a software developer with deployment experience, highlight things like "participated in deployment for releases," or "helped writing scripts for database updates" in your resume. If another job posting specifies software developer with testing abilities, highlight things like "helped create test cases," "supported and participated in user testing," and so forth.

A cover letter is sometimes recommended along with the resume. There are numerous samples online that you can use to create a simple letter, but don't forget to customize it every time you send it: Highlight things that are close to the job description, and send it to a specific person if possible.

Whatever you do, do not lie in your resume. Most companies run background checks and if they find you've been untruthful, they oftentimes will fire you immediately.

They want my head?? How headhunters work

Once in a while you might be contacted by a headhunter, or recruiter. These folks are paid to find the right person for a specific job. They are hired by the company with the job opening.

If they find you and you get hired, the headhunter company (or individual) will get a bonus. So their interest is to place you. They will give you details about the hiring managers, coach you and give you advice, maybe even re-do your resume if the company prefers a certain format.

A good headhunter can be a blessing and will find you a great job. You can try and find a headhunter on LinkedIn, where there are groups for folks looking to place applicants. Most headhunters will work with senior positions, but it is worth trying even for entry-level jobs. Ask your network if they can recommend someone. If you connect with recruiters you like, keep in touch with them for future jobs.

Unfortunately, there are also a lot of folks who claim to be headhunters but are not. They prey on applicants without much experience. Here's how to protect yourself:

- A real headhunter will NEVER ask you for any money. They are paid by the company, not by job applicants like you.
- A real headhunter will never ask for your social security number, credit card, ID, or bank account information. These are only provided to employers after you get the job, when the company needs to verify your identity.
- Real headhunters will have a website with clear contact information and a phone number. They will have job listings with enough detail. If someone contacts you from a personal email with a mysterious job offer from a secret company, with a secret salary, they are not behaving like professional recruiters.

Interviewing for the Job

Interviews in the new I.T. industry usually have three parts. First, you will get a phone call from a recruiter--either someone in the company's HR department or a paid headhunter.

This first phone interview is called 'screening'. It means your resume caught someone's attention who'd like to find out more about you. This interview is all about first impressions. Be prepared to discuss your background, and answer any questions about your resume and cover letter. Be short and clear in your answers, and do not give away too much information if it's not needed.

If all goes well, you'll get a second interview. This means you are one of the few candidates selected, so you made it out of the first round. The second interview is usually with the hiring manager directly, sometimes along with other folks on the team. This is your chance to shine.

The second interview can be over the phone or in person. If it's over the phone, prepare for at least a

30- minute (if not longer) discussion. So find a quiet place where you can use a speaker phone to make sure you don't miss anything.

If the interview is in person, dress appropriately; that is, wear a dark dress or suit with a solid-color shirt and minimal jewelry. Do some research on the traffic conditions expected during the time you'll be travelling to your interview, and determine whether and where there is available parking. Make sure you know where to go and how to get there. If you have time, do a dry run to see how long it takes you to get to the location.

In the army I learned to always be on time! So what I like to do when going to an interview is get there at least 30 minutes early to make sure I account for any traffic problems or parking issues. Then I go to a coffee place that I've scouted beforehand and have some tea or coffee, relax and mentally repeat what I want to say about myself. Then I go to the bathroom to make sure my hair, my makeup and clothes look good, This way I have some time to pull myself together, so when I walk in I look my best and I am feeling good.

The second interview is all about your job skills. The best advice I can give you is to discuss projects you worked on. Give details about the project scope, methodology, and impact. It could be a personal project or a volunteer project; it doesn't matter, as long as you can enthusiastically discuss it and your contribution to it.

For example, if you're asked, "What was your process when writing requirements in an Agile environment?" you could answer something like: "I have worked in an Agile environment when developing my project for ACharity.org. The way I wrote my requirements was as user stories, The project dealt with helping to find missing pets, and they had this really complex database..." When you discuss the project and how specifically you wrote your user stories for it, everyone understands it, and it becomes more interesting that answering, "I wrote user stories."

I also recommend strongly that you carry some samples of your work. A sample user story, use case, diagram or map from each project you worked on, that you can easily bring up as you discuss the project.

Be sure to look people in the eye as you speak. Appear confident and knowledgeable. Do not forget to ask questions: This is your best chance to find out details about the job, the company, and what the problems are. (Everyone has problems!) One question I like to ask is, "Can you tell me what some of the main challenges are in this job?" Jot down some notes for later reference.

Sometimes there are also behavioral questions. Look these up on the Internet for some examples. Practice responding to some of these at home so you can have prepared answers for questions such as, "What was your greatest accomplishment and how did you achieve it?" or "Tell me about a time you faced an obstacle at work and how you overcame it." Discuss actual details from the projects you worked on, and you will prove your experience and enthusiasm.

If all goes well, you might get a third interview, although this is usually for more senior positions.

This interview is usually with the hiring manager's superiors, so you need to step up your game.

This interview is not about your job skills. This one is to determine what value you can bring to the company and whether you can think strategically enough to be a good asset. You have to expect behavioral questions in this interview, Think of scenarios where you helped save money, save resources, speed up delivery time, or successfully dealt with a conflict in your team. These are the kinds of leadership behaviors that will be measured.

My best trick for this interview is to walk in with a lot of confidence, as if you already have the job. You need to speak of your strategic approach to the job and how you will improve the bottom line. By now you know some things about the organization's problems (since you asked them at the second interview), so you should have some suggestions about how you can alleviate its pain points by doing your job.

No one is calling! What Am I Doing Wrong?

If you don't get any calls after posting your resume, then your resume is weak. Get a resume writing professional to fix it.

If you get several first interviews but they never call for a second, you are saying something wrong. Ask a friend to listen to you when you talk to a recruiter and see what you are saying to turn them off.

If you get a bunch of second interviews but no thirds and no offers, then you come off wrong in the face-to-face situations. Again, check with a friend and practice a mock interview at home to get some constructive feedback.

It takes months for even the best, most experienced I.T. people to find a new job. Do not be discouraged if it takes a long time. Use the time to create even more projects that you can brag about. Finding a job is like finding someone to date. Sometimes they like you, but you don't like them; sometimes you love them but the feeling's not mutual. And no one tells the whole truth in the beginning. The match simply has to work for both sides to ensure it will be a good, productive, satisfactory job fit.

Final Note

Check out our website for more books in this series and for ideas, articles and more suggestions. You can also contact the author and read about others' experiences breaking into the new I.T.

The new Information Technology is no longer for geeks, math fanatics, or video game-obsessed nerds. The truth is, I.T. has now taken over everything in our lives and in doing so, it has created new jobs requiring all kinds of skills and abilities.

You do not need a computer science degree to get an entry-level job in I.T. that pays well and offers benefits. You do not need any expensive certifications or courses. You need passion, ambition, this book to help you get started, lots of hard work and a bit of luck.

Here's to your success!

--- The End ---